Dedication

To Pat and Ollie

Thank you for being my anchor in this world

The Bathtub

She sat in the bathtub a lot.

She sat there working out life's problems, or reading a good book, or talking herself down from an emotional cliff. Or at least that's what she told people. In truth, she sat there trying to start over. She could step in the warm water, suds bubbling, and pretend that certain things in her life went a different way.

That one night when she was seventeen and snuck out to the lake, she could have stayed in that night instead.

She could have spoken with more kindness and maintained her composure in the many fights she had with him.

She could have left that bottle up in the cabinet and decided that that was not a choice to take into her own hands.

She could have told the truth more, or ate healthier, or even enjoyed the nights she spent crying instead.

She could have done a lot of things differently.

She could have done a lot of things perfectly. And for that short amount of time, she does. She takes back those things and begins something different. She smiles in that warm tub.

Then the moment always comes where the water isn't as warm and the porcelain isn't as comfortable. The moment comes where she has to pull that plug and let all those imaginary moments go down the drain. She has to step into that cold air, wrap the towel around her, and know that tomorrow can't come soon enough. She can leave this reality, just for a few moments and enter a world where it's warm, perfect, and happy.

The Piñata

They had surrounded me, their eyes hungry. They had gluttony in their hearts and aggression in their eyes. There was nowhere that I could run. I was immobile and tied to a post, hanging above them like a piece of meat. They had dressed up for the occasion; it was a ceremony. I thought to myself, "How dare they? What gave them the right to take my life?" I even thought further about God. Why would he allow this ritual to continue? The ring leader edged forward, taunting the others, threatening to put me in my place. He covered his eyes, mocking me further. He carried a weapon, one that I had only heard about from the others in tales from our past. It was wooden and solid and he became familiar with the handle as he edged closer. Another hung onto the rope inching me up and down above him. I was a game to them, no humanity left within their greedy little hearts. They laughed as he swung. There was no connection and I let out a sigh, thinking maybe he would continue to miss, but my hope was dashed as another blow headed towards me. I felt the

rip go down my side. I hung there, limp, hurt, and hanging on

for dear life. He ripped off the blindfold, and with a grin,

pounded on my lifeless body as I fell to the ground. I saw them

feasting on my insides, as my eyes closed and my last breath

was exhaled. The stories were all true, I thought, and just like a

candle, I was extinguished.

The First Date

He sat down at the table. Being the kind of person that she was, she looked down at her belly that wouldn't quite go away and let out a soft sigh. She quickly brushed this insecurity away and put on her fake smile, greeting him. His hair was slicked back and his smile was wide and brightly white. She noticed how well built he was when he first walked in the door but couldn't possibly think that he was here for *her*. Although she knew that he was completely and totally out of her league, she started giving herself a pep talk before they could enter into a serious kind of conversation. "Listen, Becca, you've got a lot going for you. You have a great job, it just so happens that that job comes with a lot of business meetings with lots of leftovers. You're fine, you'll lose this weight sooner or later." And with that, they began chattering away.

In the first few minutes, she had learned that he owned a local health club down the street, he was a vegan, and he wanted to start filling her in on all the details of it.

"Oh god, he's one of THESE guys." She thought to herself. Now it all made sense. She knew there had to be a reason that he was single and interested in a blind date with her. This was the exact reason. He was obnoxious. They began talking some more. She conveyed how her job required a lot of lunches and dinners with her clients and how she had not been able to "take care of herself" since being promoted. She had to focus on what was best for her future...and right now that was her job.

"Well you know, if you want to truly focus on your future, getting down to a healthy weight is where you should start. I mean, there's nothing better than looking your best." He stated, smiling at himself. To him, he thought he was being helpful. To her, she was insulted.

"Excuse me?" She added, bringing up old feelings of being the overweight child in her prepubescent classrooms.

"I just mean that if you were to take the time and work on losing some of that weight it could be beneficial to your health."

This was her first date with this doofus and he was lecturing her on what to eat? They hadn't even ordered their main courses yet! She scoffed, thinking maybe he was that moronic and didn't understand that what he was saying was hurtful. She propped up her menu, analyzing it more closely, but mainly to block out his face. The waiter came by and asked for their entrees.

"Yes, I'll have the beetroot salad with the dressing on the side, and can I get a few lemons for my water?" She rolled her eyes at his obvious choice and smirked.
"Yeah, I'm gonna have the chicken parm, extra cheese..." She stared at him down as she said this, "and let me get another glass of the white wine please." If she was going to put up with this date, she needed a good satiated buzz and some delicious dinner. She might as well have fun with it in the process.

As the waiter walked away, he was obviously offended.

"I can't believe that you would eat meat in front of a vegan. It's a little rude." At this, she had had enough. He was definitely

NOT "the one", she knew the moment she saw his big bleached teeth and his vacant smile.

"Listen buddy, I may not be primped from head to toe and I may not eat the foods you eat, but I like eating them. I'm not going to sit here and pretend to eat a salad when what I really want is a huge rack of ribs. The chicken parm is just here to hold me over. I may not look the way you do or have the sense of self-righteousness that you do, but I'm going to enjoy every minute of my life...even if that means I get a muffin top in the process. You can leave now, I'll pick up the check. I would rather sit in the middle of this restaurant ALONE than spend one more miserable minute looking at your fake tanned ass." She finished it with a smile. He had obviously never been told off before. As he got up, a shocked expression on his face, he turned to look at her once more. He was about to say something, shook his head, and exited the front door.

The waiter's timing couldn't be more perfect. He came by with their two plates and said, "Ma'am, will he be back for his salad?"

Becca, eyeing her dinner, replied, "No, sir. He will not." She took a huge bite of the entree and continued, "But I would like to send that salad back to the kitchen and get the cheesecake instead. It looks divine."

I'D RATHER BE A WEED

What are weeds? They have color, stem, and life. Who hasn't picked up a dandelion, made a wish, and cast it away into the wind, as if the universe could somehow make it possible? They provide hope.

What are weeds? Simply a willful flower, with a mind of its own. It's determination to take root, make change happen. It locks itself into the ground, only to come back over and over again determined to take root once again.

What are flowers? Pretty, useless things. Providing occasional insight with the, "He loves me, He loves me not..." Only later, to provide despair when the answer you are searching for is not offered.

                                        As for me,

I'd rather be a weed.

Hello

It was a night like this that she craved. The one where the weather was sweet against her skin and the breeze was cool and needed. The sun hung over the mountains with the yellows and oranges hovering beneath the clouds. She stood on her balcony, admiring these colors through the trees as she sipped her lemonade. It was time for a car ride, she decided. She only wanted those 20 minutes. Those 20 minutes where the sun still illuminated the surroundings, but it hadn't technically become darkness. Dusk held a kind of happiness for her.

She grabbed her keys off the counter, locked her front door, and headed down the stairs to her car. Before she even started it, the window was cranked down to reveal the breeze she had left on her balcony. As her car shifted into gear and it purred to life, her 20 minutes had begun.

The sun was glowing over the horizon as her car edged onto the highway. The wind whipped at her hair and felt kind on her neck. She was headed towards the mountains, away from these neon lights and towards something unknown; at least that's what she pretended. She passed street signs, speed limit markers, under overpasses, and onward inching farther and farther. If she could just get to the edge of town before the sun ducked behind the masses, she could prove something to herself. She didn't know exactly what, maybe it was just a game she played with herself, but she always felt this strong urge to leave. Maybe the urge to leave though was overshadowed by her desire to start anew...somewhere new. Alas, the mountains took hold of her sun, leaving her with the stars and the moon. Although beautiful, didn't capture her heart like dusk did and with that, she turned around.

The darkness was here. It made her city beautiful among the travelers and sightseers. It was what this town was known for. It was when this town came alive. But dusk was when things weren't quite awake here. This town was just opening its eyes for the first time, greeting her with its colors. It felt like hello to her. It felt like home, for however brief those 20 minutes were.

I HATE TIME

I despise time, and yet, I'm constantly infatuated with it. It's one of those things that perplexes and astounds. I find myself longing for moments of insignificance two hours prior, only to be disheartened that I can't grab hold of it again. It's already slipped through my fingers. I look through my memories and can only pick out certain instances burned there. The others are lost amidst a sea of memories valued highly more. But still, I long for insignificance again. I want to go back to those times I'd said I was "bored" and "lonely" and shake myself, screaming, "the world offers endless adventures, take hold!"

So throughout my time here, and with each passing moment of my hands clicking on this keyboard, I grow bereaved; abandoned by the time that was given to me and slowly fades away. Things move forward, time waits for no one. It is the ever giving, ever taking, demon of our lives.

THAT YELLOW JEEP GIRL

Did you ever have that time in your life where you think things could have gone differently because of one insignificant moment? It's not a moment of epiphany, and it's not a moment where you were in it and you thought, "This is it. This is a turning point." It's one insignificant moment that you look back on years into the future and think, "Yep, that was it."

Mine was when I was learning to drive. I had been learning how to drive in my parent's Jeep Liberty and my Dad kept encouraging me to learn stick shift in his bright yellow jeep instead. I remember attempting a few times, listening to my Dad scream, "Push the clutch ALL the way in," and crying hysterically into the steering wheel. I could easily blame my Dad for not being more patient with a 16-year-old immature version of myself; however, in reality, I was a child. I had had everything handed to me. I had a wonderful childhood surrounded by endless opportunities, but I didn't see it. I didn't see it in the slightest. I look back on that moment when I gave up. That moment sitting on Silverado Drive, crying at the stop sign, knowing my father was pink in the face. I didn't know what to do at that moment, and I simply gave up. This is the first time I can remember giving up and surrendering to my doubt. After realizing that things were simpler, although unfulfilled, I was hooked like an addict and ever since then, I feel myself succumbing to the temptation of reverting back. Relapsing.

It's something that I've dealt with and have jokingly called "laziness", but it's not. Things are easier when I can make the decision to pursue or turn back. I feel in control that way and it all started in that yellow Jeep. It all started with that yellow Jeep girl...

She Wanted to Change the World

"It's a pity, isn't it?" She said flatly.

"What is?" He asked, confused by her question. Not realizing she had spoken out loud, she answered him hesitantly.

"That there is so much I want to do in the world and I won't be able to do it all." Her eyes drifted across the room, as if searching for her answer among the walls that housed photos of her true loves, maps.

"Why can't you?"

There was a long pause.

"How can you be in five places at once?" She quizzically uttered.

He smirked, kissing her freckled forehead. He shook his head, grinning, while he stared off at the map that was caked in red pins, symbolizing places she needed to go to.

"You're right, you can't be in 5 places at once," She looked down, saddened by his statement. He grabbed her face quickly, allowing her to realize that he wasn't done speaking,

"But with me here, we can try to cover at least twice the distance...and you gotta start somewhere."

She grinned, a glint of hope restored into her warm eyes.

WHEN SEATTLE RAINS

He picked her up almost everyday. She knew that he would need her most days. She was never truly fearful that he wouldn't return. It was the sunny days that worried her a little bit though. He seemed more cheerful without her those days. He would go out and not return for hours on end, coming home with a huge grin on his face and not giving her a single gesture or glance as he opened the door. He passed her, laughing on the phone with friends and planning their next outing if the weather permitted. He would look at her as he said this, a gruffness in his voice. She would shrink down as small as she could get, but knowing he saw her regardless. And with that, he went to bed, leaving her outside of the bedroom. She would look at his bedroom, thinking to herself, "I love him so much." Even with sadness in her thoughts, the next morning he looked out the window and grabbed her and she was joyful. "This is the day!" She thought this to herself as she saw the rain coming down. He was going to finally see her potential. He was going to finally take her out into the world and see the kind of love and nurturing that she gave. As he walked out the front door with her firmly in his grasp, he flipped her open, protecting himself from the rain that poured down. She was just an umbrella, loving a man, protecting him from the storm around him. As the rain hit her hard and the thunder clapped, she smiled amidst the storm...and was glad.

THE ANONYMOUS MAN

He weaves words,

tongue tied and twisted.

                                        Only able

to muddle through

                    A few sentences before a smile

appears.

Sounds won't come out.

            Noise is absent.

                                        She's

completely useless

                                        Amidst his

thoughts and words.

                                        He tells

her things

                                        Beautiful

things.

Things about the

future.

Things about the past.

Things that bind him to

her.

She's

become overwhelmed.

She's

become putty in his hands.

He's become bigger

Bigger than she intended.

She smiles,

And happiness is there.

Happiness

is greater,

greater

than she intended.

He weaves words,

tongue tied and twisted.

You're My Christmas

She laid there, staring at him while he drank his beer on the couch. He laughed loudly at whatever TV show they had stumbled upon that night. It was a simple moment. His smile that curved in all the right places. His hand that squeezed her foot every time something inconsequentially funny came up. How he would look at her through his crinkled eyes. And that was all it took. A simple moment and a Friday night in was all that it took. It was all that it took to know that he loved her. As he glanced over with his inquisitive look, he smiled.

"What?" He asked. She shook her head with a grin.

"No, tell me, please?" He looked at her even harder; his smile curving wider, his eyes crinkling harder.

"I've just been thinking about how I feel about you."He laughed and turned away, attempting to take a sip from his beer. He swallowed and asked again,

"What does that even mean? Haha!" He squeezed her foot as he always did and she sat up, leaning towards him while taking her feet off his lap.

"I just mean, I've been trying to put words to us...and I finally know what they are."

He looked at her. No words appeared.

"You're my Christmas." He let out a bellowing laugh, thinking that she was only teasing him.

"It's the middle of September!" He smiled at her.

"I know that! But you know that feeling that you get when you're at Christmas? The anticipation, bottled with warmth and comfort? How do you look at people around that time? Everything is so sincere and wonderful. It's the only time of year that magic happens."

He continued staring at her, shaking his head. He turned away, the way he always did when he had a smile too wide. It was a wonderful smile that she felt he always wanted to keep a secret. The most honest smile that she rarely saw. He turned back, facing her yet again.

"So I'm your Christmastime?"

"Yes, the twinkle in your eyes. The warmth of your skin.
The happiness in the looks you give me. You're my Christmas.
You're my tradition."

He flickered at her with that famous smile.

"Fully noted."

THE UNMADE BED

There is something hauntingly beautiful about an unmade bed. Your dreams were left there when your arch nemesis, the alarm clock, dragged you from your domain. Your warmth was left there to dissipate. Your drowsiness was what you took away. A made bed can offer order, organization, and it may even offer a good start to your day. But an unmade bed can give you more. It's a familiarity when you lay in it. There's a satisfaction provided in those ruffled sheets and the recognizable scent of your pillows. The sheets are bunched in commonplace areas, making your body disintegrate. Your body is consoled. It is what you fall into at the end of the day, encouraging you to let your stresses go and offering a moment where everything in your life doesn't need to be strategized. Then the bittersweet moment comes where you rip those same sheets off your bed and stuff them into your washer. The familiarity is washed away. The softness will be wrung out in the dryer. You'll place those same sheets on your bed in the typical fashion. You'll lie in it that night, smelling the cleanliness surrounding you, ready to make them familiar again. Ready to make them yours.

My 2.A.M.

You're my 2 AM. That's where you stay. That's where you live. That's where I think of you to reflect. I sleep deprived myself just to spend time with you...because I miss you all the other 23 hours.

As she wrote these words down on a piece of paper she realized how silly they sounded. But were they true? Of course. Staying up this late was her reflective period. She didn't plan it and it didn't really suit her lifestyle, but it was that time when the whole world around her was still. It was the time when everyone else was asleep and she could actually think her own, individual thoughts. She loved getting advice from others and she listened to it all, but sometimes to truly know how she felt about a person, a 2 a.m. time period was needed.

When people talked to her about him, she listened to what they had to say, but after a while, it began to seem like white noise.

Flaws

I have some serious flaws. Flaws that I work on everyday. They include reverting back to old habits or spending too much money, but these don't even compare to my worst flaw of all. It's my dirty little secret (that's not so secret). I hate...no...despise being single. Since I first began dating when I was 17 years old, I have never been without a love interest. That is 6 years of consistent crushes, love interests, romantic partners, you name it. That's a serious problem.

I've always gone back to previous ex's for an ego boost when I've found myself single or I've been on the hunt for someone new. Sometimes In most cases, it has been a combination of both. So I've always had someone around. What has this caused me to be? Jaded. I'm jaded by men and dating in general. This is an even more serious problem.

On to the next and the next and the next. I'm the fricken' "Little Engine that Could" about dating. I think I can...see myself with him. I think I can...be with him. I think I can. I think I can. I think I can. But despite all of this, I'm currently single, forcing myself to stay in the present. I don't want my past anymore. I don't want to worry about the future. It's making me absolutely miserable and apathetic all at the same time. How can I truly find a partner with this mentality? The answer is...I can't. I think I can't. I think I can't. I think I can't.

Because I am forcing myself to look at the present moment, I do realize that I've been lying to myself this whole time. With dating, it was all about finding "The one". This mysterious entity who is supposed to come around and change it all. False. But the lie that I've told myself is that I'm lonely and I need to find "The one". This lie has manifested itself so within my DNA that I fear being lonely more than anything. But in reality, I'm not lonely. I'm surrounded by friends and family. I cherish each and everyone of them more than I could express. I may be alone romantically, but I will never tell myself this lie again.

So the moral of this: Love when you're ready, not when you're "lonely".

LIGHTEN THE LOAD

When the world closed in, she would be ready.

She would be ready to push back.

But what she didn't plan for was that there would be someone

to push with her.

To lighten the load.

To take the world off her shoulders and truly show her the

world without the pressure.

GET ME A GLASS

There's something alleviating in holding a glass of your favorite drink. The warmth that comes from holding that mug filled with coffee and milk. The anticipation you get from drinking red wine from a goblet glass. Even further, the refreshing taste of your favorite beer with just the right amount of foam coating the top. But is it just because you like the taste of these? That's definitely not the case. The truth is, we all have become acclimated to the taste of these things. No one picks up a cup of their parent's coffee when they're nine and says, "Mmm, can I have a cup?" You make that face (you know the face that I'm talking about), shake your head, and step away from the evil drink. When we all hit college, I can guarantee that no one tried beer or wine for the first time and was like, "Ah! What a nice, refreshing drink!" In my opinion, I would've rather had some kool-aid or lemonade, but this is what all my peers were drinking, so I guzzled it down with no complaints.

But now, I can honestly tell you there is nothing quite like waking up to a good cup of coffee in the morning. There's nothing like sitting in your favorite chair with a chilled beer and your favorite TV show. There is nothing quite like being surrounded by friends and loved ones sharing in your favorite beverage. So is it about the taste? Not even in the slightest. It's about the familiarity these drinks bring. An acquaintance can soon become a friend with the offer of, "Do you want red or white?" "How much milk do you want in your coffee?" "Do you like Sam Adams?" These are all questions that we can relate to. These are all questions that provide the feeling of informality. We put down our guard and share a connection with someone just for a little while. It's the ease of cradling a cup or glass in your hand and knowing, *At this moment in time, we are experiencing the same thing and no matter what we are going through, it's okay.*

I DO CARE

When people throw up their hands in a fit of anger and spew, "I don't care anymore!" it is coming from a completely opposite place. They do care. They care a lot, in fact. But I think we are all aware of this lie. This lie is a symbol of the first step of frustration. "I just don't care!" *No, but you do.*

But what if this phrase didn't have such a negative connotation? Why is it said when we want others to know we have given up? What if it was said in a fit of happiness? "I don't care anymore!" was said with a smile and an attack upon the world. What if that phrase meant that you gave up caring about things that don't matter? It could be freeing. It could be engaging. It could be...amazing. We know that "I don't care anymore" is said halfheartedly when it is used negatively. What if it was said halfheartedly, but positively? People would know that we care about things that matter, but we've given up on things that don't. Hateful words erupted from angry people would be left behind us. Impatient people trying to ruin our morning wouldn't phase us. Bitter looks from insecure people would be dust... but why? Because we just don't care anymore.

The Supporting Character

In many and most cases, the supporting character provides a lot of things. It provides insight to the main character's personality, into their needs, and sometimes even into their past. You get a feel for the main character because of this person, and although they do provide this value, they are not what the story line navigates around. There is someone else that you are rooting for. There is someone else that you want the happy ending to happen to. There is someone else that your thoughts circulate around. But, as there always is, there is the supporting character. The high strung best friend. The quirky best friend/roommate. The nosy but good intentioned co-worker. You don't root for these characters and you never find out who they truly are as people. They have their facade's and their well mannered nature, but nothing more. You see a smile. You see a grin. You see their inquisitive eyes.

What happens when you find yourself as this supporting character? What happens when you are only seen as far as people care to see, then the camera pans away? You're there, but you're not really there. I'm starting to see myself as this supporting role rather than the protagonist. Not to anyone in particular, but in general. People are panning over me. And here I am, screaming into the camera.

KARMA KAFE

Penelope knew that she had fallen asleep. It was apparent. The last thing that she remembered was lighting a candle and snuggling into her clean sheets with a book gripped between her hands. However, where she woke up was not her bed. She woke up in a diner with yellow plastic booths and waitresses that seemed incredibly too happy to be there. They had on white aprons with their hair in tight curls on top of their head. Accompanying their outfits was a notepad and bright red pens. Penelope glanced at them closely as they strutted about the busy diner. She looked up, surprised that her waitress had crept up so quietly to her booth.

"Hello, welcome to the Karma Kafe."

Excuse me?

"This is the Karma Kafe. There are no menus, you get served what you deserve." She ended her catchy phrase with a tight grin and quick jot down on her notepad.

I don't understand.

With a quick smile she said, "Don't worry hun, we get this all the time. I'll be back in a moment." She whisked herself away, shouted something at the chef and disappeared into the back.

Penelope was confused. At first, she was positive that the Nyquil had gone straight to her head, but that thought slowly faded. She sat there and pondered what the waitress meant.

You get served what you deserve. The sentence played over and over again. She knew what karma was, and she knew she didn't like it.

Oh god, she thought. Every bad thing that she had ever done ran through her head. That one time she had smoked weed with that random guy. That one time she slept with her friend's boyfriend. That night she got too drunk to drive home, but did anyway. It was the feeling she got in the pit of her stomach when she heard her mother scream her full name.

"Penelope Leigh Hughes!" She could remember it all so vividly. The anticipation of walking down the stairs to greet her mother's face was riddled with disappointment. This was the exact same feeling. She knew that when that waitress came back, she would be greeted with the same fate. She went over every bad thing she had ever done. She had her mental list noted.

She glanced over at every flicker of movement that came from the corner of her eye. It had felt like years. Finally, just like before, she was shocked to find the waitress hovering over her.

"Here you go, doll."

She sat down for some Neapolitan Ice Cream in front of Penelope. Curiously, Penelope poked at it, half expecting worms and maggots to fall out of it.

What's wrong with it? She asked.

"Nothing, you get ice cream. That's what the notes say." She glanced at her notepad as if verifying she had served the right customer. "Most people would be relieved to get what you got." She continued.

I'm appreciative, don't get me wrong, but I don't think I deserve...this.

The waitress looked stumped and sat down next to Penelope.

"Let me guess, when I told you what this place was, you went over every bad thing you've ever done, correct?"

Yeah.

"Did you go over every good thing?"

No.

"Not surprising. Believe me, this is good. This is what you deserve."

Let's Talk About the Weather

He seemed to have a sixth sense about her. He knew when she happened to be alone, happened to be reminiscing about the past, happened to be looking down at her phone. He would always take that opportunity to pop up in her life and onto her screen. It wasn't necessarily unwelcome. It wasn't necessarily a relief either.

It was what it was.

She would look down at that phone and see the curvature of his name. The name she used to scrawl across pieces of paper at her desk. The name that meant art to her. The name that meant her awakening. The name that was the envy of her because she wanted it badly. After the initial impact to her heart, she would open that text and read.

The naturalness of his words, but the reserve that those words held. She would run her hand across the glass on the screen, hoping that some way this would make him a physical presence in her life. Their imprisonment within the memories of one another were the cards that they had been dealt. They had learned to live with the white noise of one another.

All it read was, *So it's supposed to rain here this Saturday.*

"Why do you do that?"

Why do I do what?

"Are we really getting to the age where weather is the most interesting thing we can talk about?"

I don't know what else to say. Pick something.

"No. Weather's fine. Weather has always been fine."

Resolution

Be unwavering.

Be honest with me to a fault.

Sit with me on the couch and play with my hair.

Share your thoughts with me.

Tell me your innermost secrets and then let me be the

judge of them. Trust me   enough to be yourself, and I

will do the same.

Buy me Neapolitan ice cream and know me well enough to

only eat the strawberry.   Let me make you breakfast,

even if it's 6'o o'clock in the evening.

Scan my bookshelf for a new read.

Tell me when you make mistakes.

Be self aware of your own actions.

Be kind beyond compare.

Kiss my forehead when I'm sad and kiss my hand when

I'm happy.

But most of all, love me without fear of your past because that's

what I deserve.

The Perfect Scream

I went on a road trip...*by myself*. I did this for a multitude of reasons. The main one being a quiet refresher into nature. Not only did I **not** get what I was searching for, but I got the exact opposite. Don't get me wrong, it was amazing and beautiful, but Zion was packed full of people going on vacation, happy couples eating lunch on rocks, and I didn't do any serious hiking.

So on my 2 and a half hour drive back, sitting behind the biggest tractor trailer I had ever seen, I felt this overwhelming urge to scream. Maybe that's what had been my serious draw into the middle of nowhere in the first place; maybe a subconscious feeling of needing to let it all out. However, I wasn't able to do it without looking like a total crazy person.

Staring at a license plate on a truck full of construction supplies (from what I can assume), I was trying to talk myself down from yelling. Why? Why couldn't I just do it? There wasn't anyone around me to judge. I was alone in my car listening to the loudest possible music imaginable, but I still couldn't do it. This is what my life has done to me. I put on a show, 24 hours a day. I can't even be myself by myself. Isn't that crazy? I've catered to too many people and I can't even scream in the privacy of my tinted vehicle.

But, alas, as I was switching lanes to pass my "Final Destination" nightmare, I finally did it. I screamed louder than I thought I could. It filled the entire car. I felt the thundering scream pressing against the windows. I felt...good and I was relieved. Even if it wasn't what I was searching for, it was what I found. A simple, perfect scream.

CRINKLE

The maps were strewn across her bed. The lines in red dictated where she was going and the green lines were drawn over indicating where she'd been. However, when the colors mixed together, they made a disgusting brown color, not the kind of aesthetics she was planning on going for. She was frustrated to say the least. Not about making her maps "pretty", but how she felt that no matter how far she climbed, no progress was being made. She sat on top of them and heard the distinct crinkle as her exhales coincided with the spring bed frame. She put her head in her hands, inhaling sharply. Crinkle.

CAN I EXPLAIN SOMETHING TO YOU?

For the better part of my life, I've explained things. Things ranging from "epiphanies" I've had or how "in love" with my latest boyfriend I was. But for now and for the first time, I have no explanation. I have no epiphanies. I have no juicy details. And this is something so indescribably good. I smile. I tear up. I look away. Because this is something that I'm feeling at this moment...it's mine. It's precious and it's mine. I have nothing to prove and no explanations to formulate... and that's good.

suddenly do.

Unrequited love has become convenient to keep,

and love that should have flourished has been thrown away

for reasons

for concerns

for reasons that aren't really reasons.

Temporary.

It's a bump in our path.

It leads us to our end goal.

if we

could just let it go.

let go of the temporary.

temporary is a tick.

temporary feeds on us.

temporary sucks us dry until there is

nothing.

we shall not be consumed by the temporary.

flick it away.

we do not owe it.

we do not deserve it.

we shall overcome

temporary.

temporary is a ghost.

When it is known,

it flies away.

It is swallowed up.

Las Vegas

Las Vegas has torn me open to reveal my character and spirit. Some parts I haven't truly been okay with, but I think that's part of true self-discovery; seeing every detail of yourself and being grateful for character strengths, yet mulling over and working on character weaknesses.

Every day I wake up thankful for this town, not because of what it stands for, but the way it has molded me into the person I am today. I have carved myself a backbone, ripped out that "walk all over me" mentality and become genuinely bolder. That is solely because of Sin City.

They say that you are able to find yourself after all of your trials and tribulations; that you find out what kind of person you are on the other side of that wasteland. I have. I am Katie and I'm pretty great.

I know I have a long way to go until I become the kind of woman God wants me to be, but I know (now more than ever) that being placed in Sin City was a blessing. I have reached that jumping off point and I'm completely ready to see what kind of ride is waiting for me on the way down.

Thank you, Las Vegas. You've been one large pill of tough love.

ANGER

It waits.

It sits, makes no sound.

And like a terrible explosion,

It erupts,

It startles,

It backlashes.

With no purpose

And no intention.

It waits.

It waits for her to be weak.

It waits for her to succumb.

It takes advantage of her.

It is the most hated and feared,

Feeding into those very emotions.

They make it strong.

No matter how you despise it,

It despises you more.

It uses you;

tortures you.

With regret.

It will wait for the tears to come.

It will wait for a smile to fall.

It will wait for you.

Anger.

The most patient one of all.

God?

I try to keep myself relatively transparent, so with that curse of transparency, I think it's only fair to detail what's been going on in my life.

As many people know, I was agnostic for a few years. But even during that time, I still wanted to be atheist. Even when people would ask me, "So, what are you?" I wouldn't really know how to identify myself. I would say that I didn't believe in God, but I knew that wasn't true. My belief has never really left, not even during that time.

So, here I sit, farther along in my life and my belief still stands. What people fail to realize about my belief is that although it is unwavering, it doesn't necessarily mean I'm happy with it. I'm not even close to happy. I'm angry. I'm angry at God for a lot of reasons, but the main one being this stagnant puddle I've been trapped in. Nothing changes, nothing grows, not even my relationship with him; but I don't know if I even want my relationship to grow with him right now, because I'm so pissed. I'm hurting, I have friends who are hurting, and I even have prayers that go unanswered on a daily basis. Yet... I'm stuck with this belief in someone and something that seems to not care.

Maybe this is a toddler tantrum I'm having. Maybe this is me stomping my feet on the ground, shaking my fist because I didn't get what I want, but it doesn't feel like that. It feels like I've been abandoned.

Do you remember when you were younger and that moment of panic you had when you lost your parents in the supermarket? Your first thought is, "They've left me." Then you go around, grasping at other adult's pants, thinking it's your parents, but it's no use. That's where I am. He's left me, I'm panicking, and the only thing left to do is to run around, grasping at others.

So, God... If you're there...

Where have you been?

Dye

I dye my hair to be a different person, to hopefully achieve something that I wouldn't normally achieve. It gives me courage, it gives me a mask that I can wear to be stronger than I normally am. I dye my hair to be a better person. With each color that fades, it feels like an old skin has just been shed, new colors can come into the light and be marveled at. I have a distinct feeling I was a caterpillar in my past life, waiting to form my cocoon and spread my wings to be something greater than I was. You can reach farther places as a butterfly and you can be admired for it. I try to recreate that feeling of newness, freshness, and a brighter future, simply because of a change. So I dye my hair, once again, for a new beginning.

THE MOST BEAUTIFUL VIEW

Driving to my boyfriend's house late on a Sunday night, I'm watching the sky instead of the road. I wouldn't have been daydreaming so frivolously if the roads hadn't been so barren. The super moon is out, and the clouds blocking it are abundant with a storm rolling in. Speeding around a curve, a small green Toyota passes me on my left side with a small hand appearing from behind the steel door. Their hands are dancing with the wind. She makes motions and waves with the air. As I match their speed, I see an unsurpassed grin from behind heavy bangs. She's laughing now, a heartfelt laugh that she shares with the driver. They speed ahead now, with me being the only witness to their unadulterated moment of pure happiness. In the distance, clouds rumble and lightning strikes, with that same small hand dancing in the headlights.

I AM POEM

Sitting in class the other evening, we were prompted to create an "I am..." poem. Although the example given was rather cheesy and artificial, I felt impacted to write something truthful and honest. You can find yourself in a poem, when grasping for ideas and exactly the right word. It's not much, but it definitely applies to my Tuesday.

I am passionate and troubled.

I wonder where I'll end up.

I hear the flapping of airplane wings.

I see the mountain heaving.

I want to redo loving.

I am passionate and troubled.

I pretend I am in a far off place.

I feel colors appearing.

I touch a soul departing.

I worry I'll be alone.

I cry for my regrets.

I am passionate and troubled.

I understand I am where I'm supposed to be.

I say I believe in people.

I dream I am influential.

I try to stay positive.

I hope for a smooth day.

I am passionate and troubled.

I might be anxious and unaware.

I could be unsettled and astounded.

I should be content and hardworking.

I want to be calm and collected.

I need to be versatile and corrected.

I am passionate and troubled.

INSTANTANEOUS

"I hope you find someone who can fix things instantaneously."

Those were the words that I was left with as I hit the end button on our phone call. It wasn't as if I hadn't realized this already. It was something that has always been nagging at me, but I hadn't been able to verbalize my impatience and anxiety with "time". There's too much of it and infinitely so little. It's really cliche, I know, but it's a cliche for a reason. I've always believed that.

I'm not sure where my anxiety with "time" came from, but it seems to have progressively gotten worse over the years. When it comes to an itinerary, I need to stick to it. My poor friends have dealt with this anxiety progressively over the years, but in the past few months, I've struggled inherently.

It finally hit me as those words left his lips. *Instantaneous. I need someone who can fix things instantaneously.* I replayed it over and over again.

I couldn't decide at the moment if it was a good or a bad thing. It felt bad, but maybe it had to do with the connotation that he used it in. Maybe it had to do with the situation I had put us in.

I still can't decide if my need of time to be in a correct order (and if it's not, fix it) is something that can be deemed as flawed, however, I do know that this anxiety it is causing me has been negative. It needs to change. Self-evaluation is imperative in order to progress and become the person you are supposed to be. So, here I am, self-addressing my anxiety.

1, 2, 3, go.

She Was Bound

She closed her book and stared at the wall. That's how she ended every book, with a moment of pure silence and nostalgia. She had nostalgia for a life that she hadn't lived and for a love that didn't happen. She didn't mind it though, she lived through someone else and that was enough for her. As far as her real life was concerned, that was another matter. She was a fun girl, on the outside. She was what was known as a "yes man". She would never turn down a beer with an acquaintance and she would never say no to those closest to her. She was busy for most aspects of her life, but those few and far between moments when she could be alone, she enjoyed the quiet and relished in the ideas of others. Books were dissected and movies enthralled her. She loved living their lives for the small moments of the day.

To others, she seemed to have everything. She went to school, went to work, but there was always something missing. That love that she felt in the books and movies never emanated in her actual life. All of her relationships had that failing moment that finalized with, "Katie, you'll have to live in the real world sometime." She would shake her head and run off with one fleeting question, "why?" She never understood why her hopes and dreams of her personal life seemed so far away to others and not to herself.

So then she would go back to her books and her movies. Moments that she could feel that lasting love, that nostalgia, and that hope. But maybe that was her problem. She was in love with fleeting moments. Maybe that's where she saw the most beauty. The moment where the protagonist and antagonist meet, or when the heroine falls in love for the first time, or when you find out that the person she hated was the person she loved all along. She was in love with fleeting moments bound by credits and entry music. She was bound by quiet moments and happily ever afters that never existed. She was bound.

I HAVE YOUR SOCK

I have your sock. Just one. I put it on every now and then. I'll never be sure how it comes to be in my sock drawer, but without fail... It'll happen. And I'll pull out my mismatched socks and slowly put this black sock on. I never realize it until it's there...on my foot. And I stop. Just for that one moment and I look at it. It's too big for my foot though. It doesn't fit me quite right. The heel of it is what throws it off completely. It rides up the back of my heel. Nevertheless, I'll stare at it. Remembering those moments of endless bedroom chit chat and your clothes piled up in the corner. I'll remember those socks. You would throw them off as you were laying in bed. With me. I don't know how one came into my possession. But I have it. And if you ever want it back, you'll have to fight me for that black sock. That's all I have.

I WANT TO REMEMBER

Make me remember the person that I was.

The one with long, golden hair, and bright eyes.

Make me recall the feelings of new and moments of impracticality.

Just...make me remember.

How Did I Get Here?

I have holes in my soul. Places that have been etched and drilled away. My soul is rough and grated and battered. It doesn't have the shiny gloss that it once did. It has run away from me, tired of the torment, leaving me with a dark mass. It makes me unaware of my surroundings. Without a soul, you're done. My soul is somewhere, hunkering down for the cold winter. It's waiting for my hatred to leave, so it can slowly start to heal. It has run away from me. I've treated it badly. Drowned it in whiskey and tears, trying to smother it. I don't deserve one. I never did.

THE BREAKING POINT

I walked into the DMV, painfully aware of the stares that radiated from the other's faces. I know that the colander was unnecessary, but I also knew that my thoughts were unsafe. No matter how hard I tried to get the voices to quit pestering me, I failed entirely time and time again. They told me that the others would get in. They told me I wasn't safe. So I stood in that line, my eyes flicking back and forth between the person in front of me and the person behind.

"Please, take your number."

The voice startled me. It echoed throughout the lobby of this place. *Move quickly,* I thought. *Move through the line.* I grabbed the number, and there I stood waiting for my turn to be called. The voices grew louder, telling me to stomp my feet. *It'll save the world,* they said. I did. I stomped my feet loud as it vibrated the floor beneath me. *Hit your head*, they said. *It'll save the world.* So I did. I banged on the colander as loud as I could. People began staring at me. *Shh. I know. They don't understand that I just saved the world.* I muttered this. I screamed. I forgot my volume settings. I flicked the colander one more time to adjust it. *There we go*, I muttered again. *You know what else would save the world?* They said, A *quick slice to your throat.* NO! I muttered this loudly. There must be something wrong with my volume. I'll have to tinker with it once I get home. Finally, my number was called. I stood there, my eyes focused on the camera in front of me.

"Ma'am, you'll have to take that off."

I panicked.

"But you'll see my thoughts. You'll hear them. They're not good thoughts."

She looked worried now. What if she was already aware of them? She shook her head and counted down.

"3, 2, 1…" The flash went off. They have my brain.

I SEE HIM

I see death.

He stands on the street corner, dressed in black, while I wait for my

red arrow to become green.

I see death.

He's looking right at me.

I squint and see no distinct face.

He knows me.

He sees me.

It'll be over soon.

I saw him, I just didn't know it would happen so soon.

Forgetfulness

It is hard to be thankful everyday. This is the truth we are all well aware of. However, my struggles go beyond that. It goes beyond that of trying to remember or being foggy around them. It goes into full blown forgetfulness. I wake up manic or I wake up depressed, there's rarely an in-between. I don't think people realize the full extent of my inner-psychosis. I rarely thank my friends for the impact that they've had on my life. I rarely thank my parents for their unending understanding. I rarely can think of a moment where I've selflessly loved another. But at this point, I would like to take the time and opportunity to thank these people in my life, selflessly. I've played the victim for quite a while. "Where's my person, where's my happy ending?" I've forgotten that I can have a happy ending without someone standing next to me. I have friends and I have family who I believe would do anything for me, selflessly. Here I am to do the same. Thank you all for your wonderful patience, kindness, and unending love for me. I will do better. I will show it better. I will be a better Katie to you. Unassuming and

uninhibited by my own insecurities.

CLINGING

She clung too fast.

Her nails are digging upon the wood of their relationship.

She scraped and left indentions upon the tree,

Particles trapped beneath her nails;

All signs of her disregard and contempt for

transition,

moving,

changing.

She clung too fast,

facing resistance and the rough edge of a sword.

The sword he would cut her down with,

The sword that would ruin her pedestal.

The sword that would equalize her.

She clung too fast.

But the wood was getting bitter

And cold,

And dead.

It was being ripped up by the roots of his neglect.

The roots were no longer wedged deep within the earth.

He would be blown away,

Her with him.

Or she could let go.

My 4:31

Many nights, I wake up to the sounds of cats pouncing, outside noises, and random frivolities. But the past few nights, I wake to my own feverish brain's movements and anxieties. I wake to nothing in particular, except myself. I can set my heart on that 4:30am. That morning, I woke up to a moment of no particular importance but my own heart's beats and the endless scans of my eyes across a dimly lit bedroom. I am alone. My heart is screaming through my chest. *Bum bum bum.* I will lay here until the sun cascades across my curtains. When I can no longer forget a new day has begun.

I set my heart on 4:30am. When no one is awake and the sun hasn't peered over the mountain peaks. I am that dawn. I rub the sleep from my eyes...or at least until the clock strikes 4:31.

ERRATIC

I will never understand the purpose of vulnerability. When I give

into that mindset, my entire irrationality and erratic behavior lends

itself to that very vulnerability requested from the other. I don't

want to be vulnerable. It's a place that I don't want to go to again.

I've put up walls for a very long time, hence the absence of a long

term relationship in my life. And as soon as I knock them down or

finally give into something more than just "dating", the other person

spits in my face claiming some type of newfound bullshit in which I

roll my eyes and start putting those walls right back up. I'm a

goddamn Rapunzel at this point. Locking herself in a tower, built by

her own two hands. And you know what? It's getting taller with

each and every passing relationship failure. So please, ask me to

tear down my walls one more time. Ask me to show my true erratic

self. You may get it. But you should know what you'll receive:

You'll get my mood swings.

You'll get my ultimatums.

You'll get my spur of the moment dreams.

You'll get my epiphanies (that happen more often than they should)

But you'll also get a caring person with a good heart...but whose

heart is slowly filling itself with a lack of hope and a lack of care.

Do I care anymore? Not likely. So go ahead and hand me that brick.

Dramatic

She walks into the store, laughing. She doesn't notice me
behind the cashier counter. Why would she? I glance down at my
phone, excusing my eyes from her gaze. She laughs again, more
maniacally this time around. Between her chuckles she says, "and
he asks, 'did you ever love me?' I mean, can you be more
dramatic?"

THAT BOSTON GIRL

She was a petite girl, hugging the shorter end of five feet. But as she exited the aircraft, bypassing all of the "enjoy your stay" comments by flight attendants, her confidence had her two feet taller. This was the place where she belonged and the anticipation was killing her. She wasn't even halfway outside of the airport before she started smelling the Boston air. Holding onto her backpack straps, she lurched it forward, untangling her red curls in the process. She knew that she looked like a tourist. Her overstuffed backpack and heavy sweaters didn't scream "I'm from here", but she was okay with that. She knew she'd get there someday.

She hailed for a cab.

"I need to go get myself a Boston creme pie, please."

He looked at her, puzzled. It was only 9 o' clock in the morning. She assured him that this was accurate. "Yes. Pastries," she reiterated. Off they both went into her city, starting a short bout of adventure.

The time she had there was just shy of 14 hours. *That's the tricky thing about layovers*, she thought. *They're too long and too short.* So she headed back to the airport and got back on the plane, bound for Las Vegas. Her 14 hours in the town she loved had shriveled up; like the desert she was destined for. The dry, shiny city that she ached to return to, but was never meant to stay for long. She didn't hate that town, it was just that the *shiny* had worn off ages ago. She wanted the red brick and cool breeze of Boston. She wanted to be that Boston girl.

I WISH

I've been wishing a lot lately. I've been wishing people were
nicer, including myself. I wish that the people who I am drawn
towards were drawn towards me in return. I wish that there was a
sign pointing me in the direction of the person I'm supposed to be.
Most importantly, I wish I knew what love was. I haven't felt it in a
really long time, mostly because I refuse to allow myself to be
vulnerable.

SEE ME

He held her with ferocity, but gentle and without barriers. His hand ascended her neck, grabbing her hair lightly and twirling it around his finger. His breath was hot on her neck and grabbing her waist, he pulled her closer. Never in her life had she been held with desperation. Never had she felt this level of comfort. Never had she loved someone almost instantly. 2 weeks. That was all that she had known. 2 weeks of vulnerability. 2 weeks of wanting something she couldn't have and yet, here he was, lying in her bed, holding her like she had never been held before.

The more time spent, the more moments she had cherished. Her one regret? Not meeting him 2 years prior. Before the marriage. Before he belonged to someone else. The only question that remained was one. Was she doing something wrong? She ached to feel her lips against his, but she would not act on it. The physicality would bring complications. She could never ruin this. She'd ruined a lot of things in her life and this wouldn't be one of them. So, this moment, she absorbed it. She would never forget the intimacy of that very moment. The moment that made her feel loved above all else, whether it was the truth or not. From that point on, she promised to simply love him from afar. She wouldn't let him know and she wouldn't say a word.

She'd just watch. She couldn't fall more in love. So...for the moments they had together, she'd just watch his eyes. How they lit up when he smiled. The way his lips fell across his teeth as they parted when he spoke. How her lips felt as they accidentally brushed his neck. How his chipped black nail polish became a staple and how his hands grabbed her at this moment.

I love him. And I don't know when it happened.

Just shut up

I've never been one to shut up. It's a curse. I'm hardly speechless and I over-analyze absolutely everything. But on the brighter side of these pitfalls, you'll never guess my feelings towards you. I've always kept my mouth moving and the words flowing. So, why is it that people are surprised when I call them on their shit? *You're acting like an asshole and here's why.* I know I'm not perfect and I'm hardly one to pass judgment, but I'm also aware of everything going on around me. I usually get a "wow" or a sarcastic, "thanks Katie", but I'm not going to apologize for being blunt. If I'm acting like an asshole, you sure as hell better tell me. And whether you ask for it or not, I'm going to tell you too. It's how I function.

Falling in Love

"When reading, we don't fall in love with the characters' appearance. We fall in love with their words, their thoughts, and their hearts. We fall in love with their souls."

To be an exceptional writer, you have to write about something real. That's just entirely what I believe. Whether you have an abundance of drama in your life, or very little. Whether I label this blog entry as fact or fiction, I will always have a personal connection to everything that I write.

Let's

Let's climb over a chain link fence and tear our jeans on the way

down. Shouts of "just jump!" will echo through the neighborhood

and eventual return to gravity with laughter.

Let's go lay in the damp grass and wait for the sprinklers to imitate

the groundhog, popping their heads out of the ground and

showering us.

Let's explore so heavily that the makeup runs down our faces and

for a moment, we will forget our vanity and the social pressures.

Let's forget how much gas is per gallon and sit in the driver's seat,

attempting to chase the top of the mountains in the far off distance.

Let's smell the air once more, waiting for a new season to

commence and simply...be.

Can we do that?

To someone who will never read this

I distanced myself from you. No... That's a lie. I cut you off completely.

Not because I'm cruel or because I didn't care or because of any of the other excuses you could imagine. I cut you off because being your friend was just simply... hard. You physically startled and assaulted me with your words. It pained when I would hear from you. It made me ill when I wouldn't. At a certain point, you controlled my emotions to an extreme extent.

Why?

Because I had fallen for you. And it was unfair to both myself and you. I cut you off because I was a girl holding onto something that wouldn't hook back. You couldn't. And that's not your fault. And I don't blame you.

But.. Please know: what I did was the opposite of hate. I won't say what it is or what it was to me because that doesn't matter anymore. What I do hope is that you are happy. And if being happy doesn't mean dealing with me? I'll be okay with that. I write this in

hope of you stumbling across it one day... And understanding with

your silence.

INSOMNIA

It's now 1:46 in the morning and the anxiety has hit me. I have to be up at 6:15am and there is absolutely no way I'm getting sleep tonight. Tonight is one of those nights where the tears come suddenly and the overwhelming sensation of "I can't do this anymore" becomes too much. Why? Because everything has finally come crashing down, as it usually does. I'm overstudied, I'm being thrown into busy work as a senior in college, I have way too many responsibilities thrust upon me...and the utter annoyance of "I have no one to crawl to" is apparent. I'm alone. That's the real kicker in times like these. I can't curl up to someone next to me. I can't listen to words of wisdom. I can't even complain to those around me without feeling like a total burden. I want it to stop. I'm tired. Someone else takes the reins. I can't do this anymore.

GRADUATION

So I've been in college for seven years. That's a long time. That's a

really long time. And I've had this "light at the end of the tunnel"

for quite some time. Every semester I would say to myself,

"I'll get my associates soon, I'm almost done."

"You're so close to your bachelors, Katie. Just keep going."

"Just 3 more semesters..."

"Just 2 more semesters..."

Now it's finally become, "Just 1 more semester..."

I'm faced with the realization of graduation. It's almost here. I am

sliding into home plate. The finish line is in my grasp. And despite

all those metaphors ending with celebration... I'm terrified.

I've known the frustration of being in college for so long, but

despite that, I still had a path to follow. I still *knew* where I would

be next semester. And now that *known fact* is gone. I don't know

where I'm going after I graduate. I don't truly know where my path

will lead. I have no safety net. I've spent so much time focusing on that cap and gown and now freedom is staring me in the face. Now the idea of not staying in Las Vegas **is** a reality. I don't **have** to stay here.

I talk a lot about leaving, about searching for what's out there, and going on an "adventure". But putting action to these thoughts? I'm petrified. I'm frozen. Do I leave? Will I have the courage to when the moment presents itself? This is sneaking up on me... quickly. I have to figure it out before I'm standing there, diploma in hand, and a vacant smile spread across my face.

Where do I go?

CONCRETE

The concrete. Like a warm lasting

    Comfort between my toes.

      Two feet beneath.

I walk, and

Cautiously moving forward on the warm

    Surface.

It's Nights like these.

      Alone.

Ones where the heat from the ground

Cradles my toes

And

Reaches through to heat my soul.

Concrete. The unlikely lover

Across the ball of my feet.

It reaches through in these finite moments

When a person simply needs to

Feel earth

But is satisfied with a

Twenty-first century reality.

The reality?

Concrete.

      The comfort

Shouldn't live in this futuristic feature

                But it does.

A reminder that warmth can still come from below.

An Artist's Heart

Being a creative individual is a very bipolar existence. You have manic periods where all you want to do is write and draw and paint and create new things. There are other times where you look at the work that you did and want to burn it, destroy it. Looking at it simply makes you feel worthless. You are in a constant draw between what you love and what defines you. As of late, being a creative individual myself, I've lacked this manic period that I crave so much. I've painted, however, I haven't been writing extensively. At least not the way that I used to. It's frustrating. Writing and art is my heart and when I'm not doing it every second of the day, I feel like a failure. I want to pursue this life, but how can I go back and reread what I wrote and hit the delete button. When I look at the painting's I've created I want to set up a bonfire. It's that drive that I crave. It's that nonstop creative juice flowing.

Even reading this back to myself, I want to punch myself in the face. This is the artist's struggle.

Past and Present

I'm not proud of my past, but I've accepted it. I think there is a very
distinct difference that people fail to realize.

My Fire has Burnt Out

I get in these moods. The ones where I don't want to do anything, go anywhere, see anyone. My sleeping pattern becomes 10-11 hours a night... uncomfortably. It's usually brought on by a depressive episode or something going horribly wrong. But this time feels different. I feel different. I can't seem to shake this feeling this time. For the past few months, my fire has gone out. My drive. And if I do have the motivation. It's for small moments in time and I get burnt out quickly. It's not just a depressing episode... My flame is dying. And it's making me sad. I'm sad all the time. I don't want to go. I don't want my creative side to be gone. Even while writing this, I'm mulling over my writing... Thinking it's crap. It probably is crap.

I had dreams and I'm not pursuing them. I want my bus. I want my paintings. I want some followthrough.

Maybe writing this out will help. Maybe it won't. I don't know how to shake this feeling. I don't know what to do.

The Price of Choices

Choices overrun our mind, envelop our future plans, and inhibit us from moving forward. There's a striking fear that presents themselves when a human is encountered with a variety of obstacles and they think to themselves, "Oh shit. This determines stuff." Well, hell yeah it does. And you have this unique power to make the right decision or the wrong one. Enter: Anxiety. What do you know of the right decision or the wrong decision at the time? We base our choices off the idea of our future we have already constructed in our head. We base them off our "gut feeling" and the feeling that your Momma warned you about when you were younger. But what happens if those choices lead you through a path that you haven't yet thought out?

Why It's So Hard to Love Yourself

It comes and goes in waves. I have a difficult time associating
success in my life with my own personal accomplishments. I
usually chalk it up to a matter of luck. However, when it comes to
my failures, I have no problem lying to myself. The disappointment
comes from within, no need to push it through from the outside. No
need to voice your criticisms. I'm already there. I disappoint myself
constantly and I have a difficult time accepting anything other than
failure.

With that being said, I have a love-hate relationship with my
human. I surprise myself with my decisions and my thought
process. I can look back time and time again saying loudly (and
usually with a hangover), "what the hell was I thinking?" I know
what to do, what not to do, but yet sometimes... I still tend toward
the latter. It's fun to do what you're not supposed to do, but the guilt
eats away at me and I'm back to hating myself once again.

So why is it hard to brush past those instances? Why do I dwell on situations where I can't change what happened? Simply put... I know better. I knew better and I still decided on the wrong one. So here I am, taking the time to tell you that even though you make bad decisions too, you shouldn't hate yourself for them. If you know better or if you knew better...good. Now be better.

There are a lot of times that I reflect back on and regret. I regret a lot in my life, but even with the hurt and the heartache, I wouldn't change those moments. Because in that instant, it was exactly what I wanted.

Well, this blog turned into a huge array of cliches, however, they're all true. And sometimes, just sometimes...cliches are cliches for a reason. Tend towards loving yourself. Steer away from hate. And even if you can't steer away from it, that's okay. Just make sure you know how to get back to the love lane.

UNTITLED

We'll never be together...

and I'll tell you why

you are a sad man

 man with intelligence

and knowledge…

Do you Remember?

Do you remember what it's like to write?

It seems as though life has been one big flow. I am sitting there, flowing in and out of people's lives, flowing in and out of my own hobbies. I dive in deep in some instances and come with amnesia to others. I think of the days when I used to read a book a week and I crave those moments. What has happened between then and now that has made me stop doing that? However, I look at my paintings and I am pleased. I paint nonstop. You can't keep me from it for more than a week.

But with writing? Oh that has been much longer. I'm disappointed that I call myself a writer when I can't even put a pen to paper (figuratively) twice in one week. Help me fall in love with writing again.

WHY I DO ART

Many times my ego is stroked when I hear the phrase, "Oh my god, I love it." But oftentimes, I hear nothing at all. Even more so, I hear it when my art doesn't sell at all. This lends an artist to believe that they aren't any good at all. So why do I keep doing it? It's for me. It's for myself. I could care less if someone likes my art these days. I do it because it makes me happy. I come home and see it hanging in the hallway and it instantly makes me realize that life isn't all bad. Life is full of color, shapes, and most importantly... Promise. I do art because it lends itself to that philosophy. The philosophy that I can create something... Even for a moment... On a canvas... And the only thing (or person) that has to care is myself and the promise it holds. I do art because I could care less what you think. In my mind... Shapes and colors come together. Contrast portrays itself upon the canvas and suddenly things line up. Life makes sense. And who doesn't want that in a world full of chaos? I do art because fuck you. I do art because of the colors. I do art because nothing else in this life makes sense until I step back and

say, "it's done."

BE SQUISHY.

What most people don't know about me is that I refer to myself as squishy. Most of the time, I refer to myself like this because of my body type or because it's my moment of self-actualization. I'm squishy. But after a few beers, one of my old friends and I were talking. We were talking about where we were headed and what our lives were like and I conveyed the truth behind my life right now. Hint: It's not good. I have many things happening to me. Not because of me. I don't have control over them...but they are just happening and I can't help but feel my life is spinning out of control most days.

But then, after I said these things to him, he said,

"You're squishy. You're soft."

I paused, (but it was a snapchat so I couldn't pause long.)

"You let things bounce off you. You're still full of love."

And at that moment, I started crying. I didn't think people noticed. I didn't think people thought of me at all for that matter, especially those who are 1700 miles away. Squishy isn't just what I thought my body type was. Squishy is the ability to be knocked down and get back up when things couldn't possibly seem to get any worse. Squishy is the ability to think and see positively when all you want to do is cry.

Being acknowledged for how you look is one thing (i.e. squishy), but being acknowledged for something you didn't know was an uncommon trait is another. I have an ability. I'm a superhero. I'm proudly squishy. I'm proudly bounce-worthy.

BLOCKHEAD

Have you ever felt like your soul needed to be replenished? I try to
do *one thing a day* that helps "perk my soul up", but lately it's
becoming harder and harder. I never thought teaching would have
this effect on me. Don't get me wrong, I love my job more than
anything. I am blessed with 185 little shits that I wouldn't trade for
the world. But in my free time, I used to paint and I used to write. I
used to write up a storm of poetic double entendres and paint until
my heart's content with whatever swirly thing landed upon my
canvas. I've been finding it difficult to do any of that lately. What I
do HOPE is the issue? I'm putting my creativity so much into my
career that I have nothing left when I get home. This is my
challenge then. Push myself to do it anyway. I sat in front of this
computer screen... on my prep, with 17 minutes left to spare.

I said, write.

My mind said, nope.

I said, write about not being able to write...you've done that before.

My mind said, that sucks though.

I said, I don't give a shit.

And here you have it. The biggest piece of shit I've written in a long time. But hey, I wrote.

It's too early; it's too late

She sinks.

Thick sheets wadded up around her.

She's awake.

It's 2:47am.

It's too early.

It's too late.

She is a piece of paper wadded up in an envelope, sealed shut,

crushed.

She is a downpour.

She is bitten down nails and cuticles.

She is despondent and ripped.

It's 2:53.

It's too early.

It's too late.

Her mind is a path paved with road markers reading, "Danger up ahead."

She keeps walking though.

Her needs seek more.

The danger.

The fight.

The desperation.

It's 2:55.

It's too early.

It's too late.

It's too early for talks of leaving.

It's too late for talks of staying.

It's 2:57.

It's 2:58.

Save me.

PATRICK

As I sit here, letting the warm water wash over me…I know I'm about to ruin it. Ruin it all by saying something stupid. Ruin it all because I can't communicate at the moment. I'm going to ruin it all because it seems that everything is all wrong…once again. I told him that 3 months is where it usually goes wrong. They start seeing me for who I truly am. But the truth is, at 3 months…it might be where I begin ascertaining the truth. I start realizing the lust fading and the reality setting in. No one will truly ever understand me. Understand the complexities: why I have insomnia. The jokes fade. The hunger grows. Materialism becomes prominent. But I don't want to ruin it. I don't want to let this go.

94533476R00069